# A PRAIRIE NIGHTMARE

*Books for Younger Readers by Pierre Berton*

The Golden Trail
The Secret World of Og

ADVENTURES IN CANADIAN HISTORY

The Capture of Detroit
The Death of Isaac Brock
Revenge of the Tribes
Canada Under Siege

Bonanza Gold
The Klondike Stampede

Parry of the Arctic
Jane Franklin's Obsession

The Railway Pathfinders
The Men in Sheepskin Coats
A Prairie Nightmare

# PIERRE BERTON

# A PRAIRIE NIGHTMARE

ILLUSTRATIONS BY PAUL MCCUSKER

**M&S**

An M&S Paperback Original from
McClelland & Stewart Inc.
*The Canadian Publishers*

An M&S Paperback Original from McClelland & Stewart Inc.

First printing May 1992

**Canadian Cataloguing in Publication Data**

Berton, Pierre, 1920-
A prairie nightmare

(Adventures in Canadian history. Canada moves west)
"An M&S paperback original."
Includes index.
ISBN 0-7710-1440-6

1. Barr Colony (Alta. and Sask.) – Juvenile literature.   2. Barr, Isaac
Montgomery, 1847?-1937 – Juvenile literature.   3. Lloyd, George Exton,
1861-1940 – Juvenile literature.   4. Prairie Provinces – Colonization –
History – Juvenile literature.   5. Agricultural colonies – Prairie Provinces –
History – Juvenile literature.   I. Title.   II. Series: Berton, Pierre, 1920-   .
Adventures in Canadian history. Canada moves west.

FC3242.9.14B47 1992     j971.242     C92-093705-5
F1060.9.B47 1992

Series design by Tania Craan
Original text design by Martin Gould
Cover illustration by Scott Cameron
Interior illustrations by Paul McCusker
Maps by James Loates
Editor: Peter Carver

Typesetting by M&S

Printed and bound in Canada

McClelland & Stewart Inc.
*The Canadian Publishers*
481 University Avenue
Toronto, Ontario
M5G 2E9

# CONTENTS

Maps appear on pages 45 and 68

## OVERVIEW
### The Promised Land

THERE WAS A TIME IN the first decade of this century when Canada was seen as a land of unlimited opportunity. This was especially true of the Canadian West, which had just been spanned by the country's first transcontinental railway, linking British Columbia with the settled East. There, some of the richest soil in the world lay beckoning the would-be farmers of Europe.

To the Europeans, and indeed to many Canadians, the land seemed empty, waiting to be filled up with settlers. But it wasn't really empty. Long before the white man, it had been the domain of the Cree, the Blackfoot, and the other Indian bands who trapped and hunted in a seemingly endless ocean of waist-high buffalo grass. When the railway was built, the Indian bands still roamed the plains; but in a single decade the wave of white newcomers would fence and till their hunting grounds, leaving only those little islands of native settlement the white people called "reserves."

As far as the Indians were concerned, the white Canadians were all immigrants. They did not welcome strangers to their hunting lands any more than the white Canadians welcomed the new wave of strangers pouring across the Atlantic – especially the Slavs from Eastern Europe.

The average Canadian was in favour of immigration, as long as the immigrants behaved exactly as the original British and French had behaved. It was the British-born that were wanted, not the men in sheepskin coats from the foreign countries of the Ukraine and Poland.

Only after the British arrived did Canadians begin to have second thoughts. Instead of reliable British farmers, they got men and women from the slums of Manchester, or office clerks from London who had never dirtied their hands in "honest" toil. The newcomers were often laughed at as inept – totally unsuited to the raw prairies.

And yet, as people generally do, they muddled through, made the best of conditions, and in the end prospered.

This is the story of one such group from the British Isles, who, on the face of it, stood no chance of making a new life in the Canadian West. And yet, after incredible hardships, most prospered. We should remember, when we study the strange story of Isaac Barr and his "lambs," that even today Canadians sometimes want to reject new arrivals because they seem unsuitable for life in Canada.

That's how many Canadians looked on the settlers of the Britannia Colony, which became Lloydminster, Alberta. How wrong they were!

# CHAPTER ONE
### ❧
## *Goodbye, forever*

L IVERPOOL, MARCH 31, 1903. Ivan Crossley, an eighteen-year-old Irish youth, stands on the dockside among the jostling crowd, looking down at the waters dappled by the spring sun, preparing to wave goodbye to the Old World.

The day before, he had been part of a similar scene before boarding the channel steamer at Belfast, in what is now Northern Ireland. His mother had prayed and wept. The crowd had sung "God Be With You Till We Meet Again." But they would never see each other again. Ivan had said goodbye to his mother forever.

Ivan was going to Canada with a party of Irish emigrants, hoping to make a new home on the Canadian prairies. He had already enjoyed a brief adventure in the New World, working on a fruit farm in Florida. Back in Belfast he had been kicking up his heels, wondering what to do with himself, thirsting for excitement, planning maybe to seek his fortune somewhere in the British Empire.

And then his mother received a letter from a relative in

*Ivan Crossley and other Barr colonists leave Liverpool, England for a new life in Canada.*

England. A pamphlet dropped out of the envelope, describing the wonders of the Canadian West. The writer of the pamphlet was a Christian minister named Isaac Barr.

Crossley wrote Barr at once and got an enthusiastic letter in return. He sent in ten dollars, as required, got back a receipt, and now here he was, preparing to board the old Boer War troopship, *Lake Manitoba,* which was standing out in the harbour, waiting for the tide.

In this spring of 1903, the original trickle of immigrants pouring into western Canada had become a flood. They came from all parts of Northern Europe. Thousands of Swedes, Norwegians, Germans, Poles, and Ukrainians – as well as thousands more from the British Isles – were heading for the promised land. Some were young men like Ivan Crossley, looking to make a start in life. Others were men down on their luck, hoping to better themselves on the Canadian prairies.

The Canadian government encouraged them to come. The plains had been empty of white settlers, but now the new Canadian Pacific Railway was ready to take newcomers out to till the fertile soil. The government proposed to settle one million immigrants between the Red River of Manitoba and the Rockies of what would become Alberta. It would be one of history's great mass movements, and Ivan Crossley was part of it.

The *Lake Manitoba* had been chartered by the Reverend Mr. Barr, whose enthusiastic pamphlet had appealed so strongly to young Ivan. The ship was built to hold seven hundred passengers, but this strange and often maddening clergyman planned to load it to the gunwales with close to two thousand – "the flower of England," as he called them.

At least five thousand people crowded the dockside that spring morning, all bidding each other goodbye. There were Boer War (1899-1902) veterans here, as well as butchers and bakers and even a few farmers – all turning their backs on Merrie England to start life over in an unknown world.

Great trucks arrived loaded with luggage labelled for Saint John, New Brunswick. Grandmothers cried and prayed – for they knew they would not see their families again. Handkerchiefs fluttered, children sniffled, dogs who were going along on the passage scuffled and whined.

Whole families arrived by carriage, toting baskets of food and shotguns, umbrellas and birds in cages. A military band struck up a festive air. The crush on the dock became unbearable.

They represented a cross-section of the British Isles – a hundred from Scotland, another hundred from Ireland – men from the coal pits and cotton mills, from the stores and offices. There were fifty clergymen's sons setting off in one group, and five offspring of one Irish peer. They came from points as far away as John o' Groats at the northern tip of Scotland and as close as the River Tweed.

Scores were dressed for the New World – or what they thought was the proper dress for the New World. They turned up in riding breeches, puttees, and broad-brimmed

Stetsons, with bowie knives at their hips and pistols at their belts. They were heading for the great Northwest, the domain of the people they knew as Red Indians. There they intended to become gentlemen farmers, living a countrified life.

The Reverend Mr. Barr had told them that their neighbours would be others like themselves – no sweaty Slavs, or German dirt farmers, or grubbing Yankees for him. This was to be an all-British colony and he would allow only proper Britons to join it.

At last the little black and white tug pushed the liner towards the dock. Great heaps of baggage were hoisted aboard. Trunks and boxes were hauled onto the deck by rope, and if some broke open spilling their contents into the sea, that was too bad. The tide waited for no one.

As the ship moved out into the harbour stern first the dock became a sea of waving handkerchiefs. There were so many people on one side of the ship that it threatened to tip over. "Get these people topside!" the captain roared up to the mate. And so the long and irritating voyage began.

Standing at the crowded ship's rail not far from Ivan Crossley was another youth, Robert Holtby. As he looked down on the tear-stained faces of the people on the dock, he felt a lump in his throat. Now he too realized that he and his family were saying goodbye forever to their home in Leeds. The chances were he would never see his schoolfriends again.

That thought was too much for him. He could no longer

bear the sight of the waving crowd, growing smaller and smaller as the vessel steamed toward the open sea. And so he turned away and went down to his bunk in the hold. When dinner came, the food was so awful that he forgot one misery and replaced it with another. Like many of his fellow passengers, he began to have second thoughts about the Reverend Isaac Barr.

# CHAPTER TWO

~

*Isaac Barr's flawed dream*

WE MUST NOW BRIEFLY LEAVE Ivan Crossley and Robert Holtby and take a hard look at the man responsible for sending them off to Canada.

Barr was one of those dedicated enthusiasts driven by a kind of missionary zeal, not to save souls, but to engage in wild projects. At a first meeting he seemed likable, earnest, and thoroughly believable. But he was not quite what he seemed to be.

His plans were impractical, his promises could not be fulfilled, his ability was less than it should have been, his organization was hollow. He was, in short, a charlatan – though perhaps he did not know it. He fooled everybody, but then he also fooled himself.

He had arrived in England from North America in January of 1902 after an up and down career in Canada and the United States. He'd been raised in Hornby, in southern Ontario, and had served as a Church of England priest in a series of posts – none of them for very long. His parishioners obviously didn't care too much for him, for they made no real effort to keep him when he argued about his salary.

In 1875 he became a missionary in Prince Albert, in what is now Saskatchewan, but he left that position too after a few weeks, on the excuse that his wife and son were both sick. He returned to Ontario and lost his job again, and spent the next two decades in the United States where he held half a dozen posts. He was obviously not a very good clergyman. He had been, by his own account, married and divorced three times – a fact he apparently succeeded in hiding from the church.

When he arrived in London in 1903, Isaac Barr was fifty-three. He had, he said, "a strong desire to take up my abode again under the old flag which I love so well." He applied for a job as a Canadian immigration agent, saying he "had some successful experience in locating people and land, and have for years taken a deep interest in immigration and colonization." That was all pretty vague. When he didn't get the job he started a scheme of his own. He would set up an all-British colony of immigrants from the old country, somewhere in the North West Territories of Canada – an area that included the present-day provinces of Alberta, Saskatchewan, and much of Manitoba.

By this time he had practically broken with the church, but he did get a licence to preach during the summer at St. Saviour's in London. This allowed him to wear his clerical collar, which gave him an aura of holiness. He himself was short and thick-set, with a broad moustache and plump features. He also had the voice of a bull, but he could also be soft-spoken, courteous, and convincing. As one of his future colonists put it, "you could not help but trust him."

Yet there were some flaws in his character. He didn't have any sense of humour; he couldn't stand criticism; he had a quick Irish temper; he tended to be a bit of a dictator. He wasn't able to share his power, and he couldn't accept the truth, when the truth got in the way of his own desires. But he certainly was imaginative, and he certainly had a way with words.

In fact, you could say he was drunk with words. He knew how to use them and he believed in their power. Once the plan took shape on paper, it was, in Barr's curious way of thinking, halfway to completion. All during the spring and summer of 1902 he had been churning out articles for no fewer than thirty-two publications. Thus the grand scheme of an all-British colony in the Canadian West began to expand in his mind.

What a triumph it would be! To place hundreds, even *thousands* of stout British farmers and tradespeople – the finest stock in the world – in a colony all their own. And no foreigners would be allowed to creep in! Barr was British to the core.

In his imagination he had already built a town. It would have shops and schools, churches and a post office, all grouped around a central park, with the farms of the settlers circling it for miles. His enthusiasm about this nonexistent city was so infectious that by August he had received two hundred inquiries in writing and a hundred calls. As a result, Barr produced a small pamphlet outlining his scheme. He said it would be cheap to build houses because building materials could be purchased in quantity. Horses, oxen, cows, implements, and seeds would all be arranged for in advance and available for purchase on the spot. And there would be openings for tradesmen and teachers, as well as farmers. He claimed that "agriculture on the prairies is simple," and that "the work is not very hard." Anyone who knew conditions in the Canadian West would have not been impressed by his words.

Barr needed an official okay for his scheme and so sent a draft of his pamphlet to the Canadian immigration office in London. He asked for its help, and also for a year's contract "and a very moderate salary," plus an office and expenses, and free transportation to Canada to choose the site of his proposed community.

Barr claimed that most of those who had called on him were either practical farmers, or the sons of farmers. That just wasn't true. And it was farmers – and only farmers – that Canada wanted. "I know the North well, having laboured as a missionary at Prince Albert in the North Saskatchewan," he wrote. That too was totally misleading. But who could check up on Isaac Barr?

Barr didn't get what he wanted at first because the immigration commissioner was away. That didn't stop him. He produced a second longer pamphlet in September, which suggested, falsely, that he was a man with wide farming experience in Canada and that he had something resembling an official seal of approval from the Canadian Immigration Department.

Here is an example of the kind of thing he was writing:

"Modesty suggests that I should not say anything of myself, but it seems necessary that I should.... First, then, before taking action I conferred with the Canadian Emigration Commissioner here in England, and I keep in constant touch with the Emigration Office, although this is a perfectly independent movement." What he suggested, but wasn't able to say, was that he did not have any seal of approval from Canada.

And then he wrote, "I was born on a large farm in Canada, and learned all branches of agriculture. With me, farming has always been an enthusiasm – I might also say a passion, and I have farmed both in Canada and the United States. I have been interested in Colonization for many years, have done some fairly good work as a colonizer, and am now anxious to build up my native Land, and keep it as much as possible in the hands of people of British birth...."

This was all hokum – but nobody bothered to check. Nobody bothered to find out how much time he had spent in the Northwest. (It was very little.) No one bothered to look into his claims to be a colonizer. Nobody even examined the list of applicants for the colony to see if they were really farmers. No one really *wanted* to know.

The British took him at face value because he was a churchman. How could he be dishonest? And Canada was eager to get more British immigrants into the West. The government had been strongly criticized because it was bringing in so many poor Slavs from Eastern Europe instead of well-to-do British farmers.

*The Reverend Isaac M. Barr (right) and his associate, the
Reverend George E. Lloyd.*

Unfortunately the British farmers were well off and perfectly content to stay where they were. It was the industrial and office workers, slum dwellers – city people unfit for the rigours of the Canadian prairie – who hammered on Barr's door.

But here was an apparently imaginative man – a Canadian and, undeniably, a man of the cloth – prepared to bring thousands of Britons, "very generally men of sufficient means," as he put it, into Canada. Clearly they wouldn't be a burden on the country. Nor would they water down Canada's sacred Anglo-Saxon heritage. The press was enthusiastic, and so was the response to Barr's pamphlets.

Now another enthusiast, also a clergyman, joined Barr. This was the Reverend George Exton Lloyd, a tall, gaunt, Church of England minister who knew far more about the Canadian Northwest. He had just come back to England after an absence of twenty years. His background was so romantic that it spurred on those who wished to follow him into the promised land.

Born in London, Lloyd had gone out to Canada at the age of twenty. He spent his first five years in the poverty-stricken backwoods of Ontario. Then he fought in the Saskatchewan Rebellion. At the battle of Cut Knife Hill in 1885, with his last cartridge gone and a bullet piercing his side, he was saved by a last minute rescue from certain death at the hands of the Crees fighting alongside Louis Riel, the Métis leader.

The Queen's Own Rifles made Lloyd their chaplain.

Later he became an Anglican minister in Winnipeg, and in 1891 he founded a boys' school near Saint John, New Brunswick. But now, in 1902, at the age of forty-one, he was back in London, as assistant secretary to the Colonial and Continental Church Society.

Lloyd, like so many of his generation, believed unquestioningly in the rightness of British causes, whatever that cause might be – even if it involved killing Boers, Métis, or Matabele. He believed in these things as strongly as he believed in the evils of alcohol, or the revealed truth of the Gospels. That is how most people thought in the early years – even committed Christians.

Lloyd was upright, relatively humourless, but certainly dedicated. And he was also a born leader, a good organizer (though an impractical businessman) – the kind of person that people instinctively liked. But he could also drive people into periods of frustration.

He didn't want "foreigners" watering down the Anglo-Saxon heritage of Canada. He wanted to take a few thousand people "of good British blood" to settle the farm lands of the west. Why didn't they go? he asked. "Are they afraid they'll be going from civilization to barbarism in a wild, unknown land?"

He had certainly struck a nerve. When he offered to answer questions, a deluge of letters swamped him. And no wonder. Britain was overcrowded. The Boer War was over. Thousands of veterans had come home. But jobs were scarce, firms were failing, and vacancies had to be made for sons coming into family businesses. Labour was cheap, wages low.

On the other hand, the Victorian age had reached its peak, and the ambition to bring British ideals to the untamed corners of the globe burned in every Englishman.

Unfortunately it wasn't farmers who looked across the Atlantic. It was the huddled masses in the cities who yearned for a return to simple rural life. Surely, they figured, their dream could come true in the open spaces of Canada.

One man who answered Barr's call later wrote, "Most of us pictured our homesteads as picturesque parkland, grassy, with gently-rolling slopes, interspersed by clumps of trees, a sparkling stream, or possibly a silvery lake thrown in, the whole estate alive with game of all kinds." But the Canadian Northwest did not resemble the fields and hedgerows of the English countryside.

Still, shortly after Lloyd himself issued a circular letter answering forty-two questions most frequently asked, Barr knocked on his door and the two joined forces. Lloyd would run an office in England and begin to take applications for the Britannia Colony, as it would be called. Barr himself left for Canada.

# Chapter Three

*Promises, promises*

ISAAC BARR WAS A HUSTLER. He published his first pamphlet in mid-August, 1902, rushed out his second in mid-September, and by early October had arrived in Ottawa from England. At the end of that month he was one hundred miles (160 km) west of Battleford, in what is now Saskatchewan, selecting homesteads for his new colony.

He returned to England in time to publish his third and more detailed pamphlet before Christmas.

Barr announced that he would bring out his first shipload of settlers in early March – only a year after his original arrival in Great Britain.

The deputy minister of Immigration, James Smart, was so impressed he agreed to reserve homesteads in eight townships until February or later. All he wanted from Barr was a list of prospective immigrants and fees to register the titles to their land.

"He is most enthusiastic and is also very clever, and I am inclined to think that he probably stands a good chance of making a success of his work," Smart said. Meanwhile, Barr had persuaded the Canadian Pacific Railway to reserve additional homesteads in the same area for sale to the British. Things were moving at a fast clip.

But there were those who were not so enthusiastic. One Tory MP dismissed Barr as a "sharper." Experienced men in the colonization field thought that he was inexperienced. The government itself remained cautious. It refused to hire Barr, give him any expenses, or set him up in an office.

The department became nervous at the speed at which Barr was moving. He was actually talking about bringing his people out in early March! That was the season when the weather was so bad that a previous group of women and children arriving in April had all come down with influenza. March was the month of storms on the prairies – the worst possible time to impress newcomers. The government urged delay. The clergyman, who didn't like anybody getting mixed up in his plans, agreed to the postpone the sailing date – but only until the end of March.

The press on both sides of the Atlantic was captured by Barr's eloquence. He had moved so quickly the government couldn't wash its hands of him even if it wanted to. He'd reached Canada at a time when the opposition party in Ottawa was demanding more English immigrants and fewer Slavic paupers. The fanatical Doukhobor sect known as The Sons of Freedom were also on the march, causing the authorities no end of trouble. If Barr were denied a chance to bring out more Englishmen there would be a public outcry.

The trouble was that Barr had let his imagination run away with him. In his new pamphlet he proposed a series of schemes, such as a "Stores Syndicate" that would operate retail stores in the colony, a "Hospital Syndicate" that would look after the community's health; and a "Transportation Syndicate" to carry the colonists and their goods comfortably from the end of the railway to the site. These weren't much more than pipe dreams.

Was he in it for the money? "I'm not on the make," he declared. And certainly profit was secondary to his grand scheme. On the other hand, he did make money: he got $1.50 per colonist from the steamship company, and commissions from the CPR on the sale of railway lands. He also planned a $5.00 charge on homesteads for those settlers who wouldn't come out with the first group. That was illegal under the Homestead Act.

But in England enthusiasm was building. Barr's newest and longest pamphlet had described his journey to Canada, and outlined the area reserved for the Britannia Colony. "Those who wish to join us must decide at once and deposit passage money," he declared. Ivan Crossley was one of those who put their money down.

Much of what he wrote was sensible and accurate, but some of it was misleading. He managed to give the impression that fruit trees – apple and plum – would grow easily in Northern Saskatchewan. Anyone who knows Northern Saskatchewan would know that that was not true. He suggested that the Canadian Northern Railway would reach the settlement "within a few months." That was not possible. Its construction would take far longer. He said timber was easily available and could be rafted downriver from

Edmonton, and that a good road existed between the railway's end and the colony. Those were wild exaggerations.

He also faked the distances. He suggested that a factory for producing sugar from beets was close by. Actually it was three hundred miles (480 km) away. Although he agreed that it was "sometimes very cold," he made a good deal of the "invigorating and enjoyable climate" and "the dry, and highly exhilarating atmosphere." But words like "invigorating" and "exhilarating" were code words for "freezing cold."

He didn't tell his prospective colonists how long the winters would be. He didn't give any details of the kind of sod, log, or frame houses they would have to build. He promised that "at Saskatoon there will be provided horses, waggons, harness and provisions for the journey, also coverings for the waggons, camp stools and other necessary things." He said women and children would go by covered wagon, stage service all the way to Battleford, "where they would be suitably housed and cared for until the men could establish homesteads."

These were paper promises, but they were believed. How could anybody living in England's green and pleasant land imagine a country where a road was nothing more than a rut, a village was a huddle of shacks, and a homestead was a vast expanse of unbroken turf stretching off to the horizon?

The English people knew a good deal about the settled cities in Canada, such as Halifax, Saint John, Montreal, and Toronto. These had streetcars and six-storey brick buildings, banks with marble pillars and theatres – even opera houses. Those who had relatives or friends in Quebec, Ontario, or the Maritime provinces also knew something about the country. They knew about the CPR with its new chateau-style hotels at Banff and Lake Louise, which were advertised throughout England. As for Winnipeg – traveller after traveller wrote of its miraculous growth, its electric railway, its brick buildings, and its block pavement. Winnipeg was the West, wasn't it?

Few Britons, alas, realized that after Winnipeg civilization came to a stop. Canada was really two countries – one half-sophisticated, the other as empty of European

*The prairies as British immigrants hoped it would be …*

settlement as the desert. In a country like England where you couldn't travel a mile without seeing a cluster of little homes, it was difficult to imagine a realm where your nearest neighbour was a quarter of a mile away, a realm peopled by nomadic natives, Métis, and a few white trappers.

Who in crowded England could conceive of the vast distances west of Winnipeg? No map could convey the emptiness, the loneliness, the desolation. And so, to most of Barr's prospects, the Britannia Colony was just around the corner from the nearest big city.

*... and how it really was.*

By the end of January, 1903, Barr's scheme had, in his own words, reached "immense proportions." He claimed he could bring out as many as six thousand settlers that March, but since he couldn't handle that number he was closing off the movement. He would settle for about two thousand.

This represented an enormous change – the previous fall he had only figured on a few hundred. The Canadian officials in London had already become disillusioned with Barr. Unfortunately, in Canada the enthusiasm was snowballing. Now the government knew it would have to step in to prevent a disaster.

Barr had sent advance agents from England to the Canadian West with instructions to scout out supplies. Unfortunately they had neither the money nor the authority to buy anything. Several members of the so-called Stores Syndicate arrived from England with big plans to start business in the new colony – but they also had very little money. In fact the Stores Syndicate did not really exist.

That was March 10, just two weeks before the Barr party was due to leave England. Meanwhile, Barr's advance agent, Charles May, who had been sent to Battleford, apparently to buy supplies, turned up in Winnipeg to reveal that he had no money to buy anything. Barr kept firing his agents. By March 19th he hadn't spent a dollar in Canada.

The Minister of the Interior in charge of immigration was Clifford Sifton, a tough-minded member of Wilfrid

Laurier's cabinet. He began firing off telegrams to London urging that Barr be brought to his senses because he was clearly misleading everybody. Without waiting for Barr, Sifton hired two farm instructors to teach the newcomers practical agriculture as well as land guides to help them find their homesteads.

The minister had lost all faith in Barr's arrangements. He sent his colonization agent, Wesley Speers, to Saskatoon to see that big tents, firewood, and fodder for the animals were spaced at regular intervals along the trail that led to Battleford and on to the colony.

Meanwhile in England, his deputy, James Smart, was trying his best to push back the sailing date. He got nowhere with Barr, but the shipping company agreed to pretend that slight repairs were needed to cause a delay until perhaps April 1.

Barr's enthusiasm had not lessened, nor had his self delusion. As late as March 21 he suggested to *The Times* of London that all of his projects were thriving. But he didn't leave it at that. He went on enthusiastically to talk about "lumber yards, creameries, mills, grain elevators, schools, post offices, and a newspaper," which, he claimed, would be set up without delay.

Barr was a man who, simply by promising that something would be done, made it a fact in his own mind. The truth was bleaker. It turned out the Indians couldn't furnish any lumber for the colony until the middle of May, when it would be too late. The Battleford contractor, who had been hired to provide portable sawmills, refused because Barr's plans were so flimsy. There was no plan for hay or oats for the horses. And Barr's brother, Jack, who had gone to Calgary to buy two carloads of broncos for the so-called transport service, found that half of the horses had suffocated to death.

In Canada Barr's house of cards was collapsing. In spite of this he was on the high seas heading for Saint John, New Brunswick, with two thousand colonists. Somehow, this idealistic, if incompetent clergyman had managed to pull off a coup. He had slithered around the cautious Canadian bureaucrats, bedazzled two thousand generally unromantic Britishers with his wild dream, shocked the Canadian government into sudden action, and bamboozled everybody into taking part in an adventure whose outcome was uncertain and, for some, would be horrific.

# Chapter Four

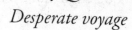

*Desperate voyage*

With close to two thousand passengers crammed into space intended for seven hundred, the voyage across the Atlantic was close to being a disaster.

The steerage passengers were divided into sections, each with its own cook: single men in one hold, married couples in others. The better off travelled in second-class cabins, but there was no first-class.

Thirteen-year-old Paul Hordern, the son of a dry goods merchant from Leicestershire, scrambled about with his father looking for their bunks. They finally found themselves in the forward hold with seven hundred others. At first sight, as they made their way downward, the setting seemed shipshape, the walls painted gleaming white. Only later, when the big waves hit and the whitewash peeled off the walls, revealing a layer of manure, did the Horderns realize that this had been a cavalry ship loaded with horses.

The murky holds, full of smoke, had two or three tiers of bunks. One second-class passenger, Stanley Rackham, visited one of these gloomy caverns to locate his vast array of luggage (he was travelling with 350 pounds [159 kg]). Now he thanked his maker he didn't have to spend much time below. What would it be like, he wondered, when the weather grew rough and people crammed into these bunks grew seasick? He shuddered to think of it and decided never to go below again.

But almost everybody was seasick. Paul Hordern was overcome so suddenly in his upper bunk that he didn't have time to shout a warning. Fortunately somebody across the way shouted, "Duck!" and the man below jumped aside, reproaching Hordern: "Why the devil didn't you holler?" he asked.

"How can I, with my mouth full?" Hordern replied. There was a six-inch (15 cm) layer of sawdust below his bunk to handle such emergencies.

Young Robert Holtby was so sick he wished somebody would come along and pitch him overboard. After a few days he recovered enough to swallow solid food, but he found he couldn't face the food in the hold, with its smell of soup and potatoes and sour sawdust, and a foot and a half (0.5 m) of bilge water slopping back and forth.

Robert shovelled some food onto a plate and went up on deck, and there he found a hundred people like himself, sniffing the salt air and trying to balance their plates on their knees.

Here, when the weather was fine, they could hear the strains of a portable organ and youthful voices singing familiar hymns. This was Miss Laura Sisley, a banker's

*Laura Sisley's organ offered a welcome break from the difficulties of shipboard life.*

daughter from London, and her charges, a dozen under-privileged boys from the church club she ran in downtown London. She had come into a small fortune on her father's death, and she was using that money to bring them all out to the new country where she hoped to settle them together in their own community near the Barr reserve.

Miss Sisley's organ was welcome, because shipboard life had taken on a sombre tone. Barr was not a diplomat. By the time the ship reached Saint John, he managed to anger a good percentage of the passengers, especially those below in steerage. One of these, Harry Pick, wrote that "it speaks well for British love of law and order to record that only eleven fights, seven incipient mutinies, three riots, and twenty-two violent interviews with Barr ... occurred during the voyage." He may have been exaggerating, but this was certainly a stormy voyage.

A lot of that was Barr's fault. He'd painted the rosiest possible picture. Now, with the reality facing them, his flock turned against him. Barr wouldn't mix with the passengers as Lloyd did, but kept to himself in his cabin. Lloyd gave regular lectures on Canada, complete with question and answer sessions. In dealing with scores of complaints, he was tactful, clear, and forthright. More and more, as the voyage progressed, the passengers looked to him as their natural leader. Barr seemed to have a dislike for contact with any of them.

What an odd pair they were. The squat, heavy-set Barr was quite a different character from the reed-thin Lloyd, with his gaunt features and his long side-whiskers. Lloyd was leaving England forever. With his wife and five children he would make his home in the new colony that would one day bear his name and be known as Lloydminster. When Barr did meet with the colonists, he often lost his temper. Once, in a fury, he threatened to turn a fire hose on them.

No sea voyage in those days was pleasant, but this vessel was so badly overcrowded that whole groups of families were squeezed together below decks with little privacy. There weren't enough lifeboats for all the passengers. And there wasn't nearly enough fresh water. The colonists had to get along on partially-distilled salt water, so brackish it ruined the tea.

The food was terrible – the potatoes rotten, the meat tough, the knives and forks dirty. There was no butter and no bread, only ship's biscuit. "We didn't die, but we damn near starved to death," Ivan Crossley wrote later. He and his comrades from Ireland sat at a long table in steerage. When the waiter arrived with a basket of hard-boiled eggs, they'd roll them down the table, the diners grabbing at them as they whirled by.

Many of the dining room and kitchen staff had signed on for the voyage, but they quit before the ship sailed, when they heard there were so many immigrants aboard. Barr had to hire replacements for them from among the passengers, but not before some ugly scenes occurred. Lloyd was called to one dining room to settle a fight involving a group of

Boer War veterans. One of the ex-soldiers had thrown a pot of jam at a waiter.

"Sure, I threw the jam tin at him," the veteran barked.

"What, a little fellow like that?" said Lloyd mildly. "You might at least help him to scrape the jam off."

With that the soldier complied and the two shook hands. Barr, on the other hand, was the kind of man who always ran from trouble. Driven half-crazy by complaints, he shut himself up in his cabin and refused to see anybody.

At one point Ivan Crossley and his friends went to Barr's cabin to demand he come down to the dining room to see how bad the food was. Barr agreed, and that night in the hold he stood up on a wooden box and tried to explain he was doing his best to improve both meals and conditions. At that point, somebody threw a ship's biscuit at him. It was three inches thick and the size of a saucer, and it hit him squarely in the nose, knocking him off the box and touching off a big fight. The crew finally rescued the clergyman, who retired to his cabin for the rest of the voyage, crying out that his people were nothing but a bunch of savages.

On April 5, Lloyd conducted the Sunday service with the ship twelve hundred miles (1,920 km) out of England. The setting provided a contrast to the hurly-burly of the dining rooms. One twenty-seven-year-old colonist, William Hutchison from Southey Green, thought it the most interesting and impressive service he'd ever attended.

It was held in one of the holds, with the men sitting on

their cots or leaning on the rails of their bunks, smoking their pipes and listening as three violinists accompanied the hymns.

Looking about, Hutchison couldn't help noticing the strangeness of the surroundings – the gun cases, coats and hats, kit bags hung on nails, boxes, trunks, bundles of rugs, and bedding strewn about. It wasn't what he was accustomed to at the Evensong services in the Anglican church back home in Southey Green.

In spite of what Barr had told the Canadian government, few of these men were farmers. The problem was that Barr was inclined to tell people just whatever they wanted to hear. This was the flaw in his pamphlets and in the rosy interviews he continued to give to the press.

The few colonists who had had some farming experience were surrounded by a group of men eager to learn what they could from them. As one remembered: "Very few had the remotest conception of what conditions actually were, or what difficulties would have to be overcome, but trusted blindly toward our leader and all his promises...."

Barr had a large map on which he invited people to pick out their homesteads. They did it sight unseen. But he said it would save time and confusion, and then he told them that the ground was so uniform that it didn't matter where they settled, because every quarter-section was like every other one. That was a bald lie.

One stonemason asked for a homestead that had enough rocks on it to build a house and Barr cheerfully agreed that this was easy to get. "I've got just the thing for you," he said and marked out a quarter-section on the map. And yet he had already told Lloyd that "not a stone will be found in the new colony that was bigger than a walnut."

The ship reached Saint John harbour on April 10, 1903, but it couldn't dock because this was Good Friday. One group got together and raised three hundred dollars to buy Lloyd a buggy and two ponies. It's hardly surprising that there was nothing given to Barr. In fact, the passengers grew angry when they learned that Barr had ordered eight thousand loaves of bread which he intended to sell them at double the going price.

"The old rogue is trying to make some money out of us," Robert Holtby wrote in his diary.

The next day, Saturday, the immigrants found they faced days of waiting while customs officers tried to inspect the mountain of luggage. And what luggage! Few had any idea of a country where vans and lorries did not shuttle back and forth between villages.

Barr had promised a transport service and they took him at his word and brought all their worldly goods to the new country. One man had brought a ton (907 kg) of baggage. Others brought pianos, heaps of furniture, and cases of books. There were bathtubs, jewellery, banjos, bicycles, gramophones, sewing machines. None of this would be of any use in the desolate land for which they were headed. But they had vast wardrobes of clothes, including formal wear, and they had parrots and canaries in cages, and, being

English, they had well over a hundred dogs, tied up on the after deck all howling to be exercised.

And then at this point, when everybody was out of sorts, Barr, unable to take responsibility, vanished. And so Lloyd did the job, going directly to the CPR, which was eager to get the trains moving. He managed to have the customs inspection cancelled, and so the ship was able to dock at five in the morning on Easter Sunday. At nine that evening, the first of four trains left for the West.

They couldn't sort out the luggage. Piles of boxes and trunks jammed the freight shed so solidly the owners couldn't squeeze between them to identify their own. Everything was piled onto the baggage cars to be sorted out later at Saskatoon – and that even included the blankets the passengers had brought with them. There was, however, a pile of blankets, which the Stores Syndicate had bought for sale, and these were piled on the dock. Lloyd doled them out to the shivering immigrants, keeping a careful record of those distributed.

And then, just before the last train left at midnight, Barr turned up, apparently drunk, and got into a screaming fight with his partner, charging that Lloyd was stealing the blankets. He even tried to sell some at four dollars apiece, but in his befuddled state, had difficulty counting the money.

Ivan Crossley watched in amusement as Barr tried vainly to make change. When Barr gave him back two dollars too much, Crossley returned it. "You're the first honest man

I've seen in the community," Barr told him. Typically, he didn't travel with his charges but left for Saskatoon on the regular train.

The two Horderns, father and son, refused to buy Barr's bread. Instead they stocked up at a local grocery, having learned that food would be hard to get on the train trip. They bought cheese, beans, and canned goods, which they ate cold because there was only one small stove on each of these crowded colonist cars, and that was used by women brewing tea.

The trains swayed so badly one night that young Paul in the top bunk was thrown directly across the passageway, tumbling onto two sleeping people. "Where'd you come from?" one of them asked, surprised.

"Leicester," said Paul Hordern, sleepily.

But the Barr colonists were welcomed by the newspapers. The *Globe* found them "a splendid class," the *Winnipeg Tribune* "a fine-looking lot, above the average." To the *Manitoba Free Press* they were "strong, manly, clean, well-dressed, intelligent."

The *Toronto News* went wild over them. It described the women as "rosy-cheeked English farmers' help, sinewy and graceful, and with a glitter of gaiety and intelligence about their eyes." The paper added that "the hands that rocked the West's cradle will be strong enough to rule the world of Canada in a few years." These papers spoke for the British-born population, who felt that the only pure immigrants from Europe would be Anglo-Saxons.

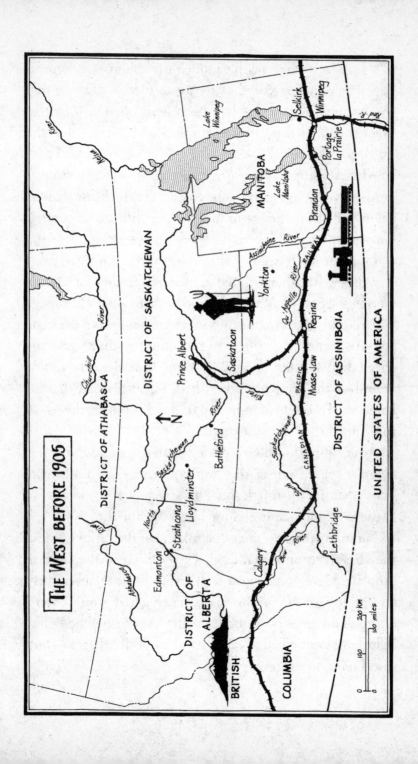

THE WEST BEFORE 1905

The government people guided the colonists to Winnipeg. There the newcomers were astonished to discover that the immigration offices had been kept open all night to greet them. At this point two hundred bachelors left the train to seek work.

After Winnipeg, the journey offered several diversions: a herd of five thousand antelope crossed the tracks and barred the way; sportsmen produced their rifles and potted gophers, prairie chickens, and rabbits, shooting from the train windows. In spite of this, the group was uneasy.

Stanley Rackham noted a general feeling of unrest among the group. What lay ahead of them after Winnipeg? They couldn't know, but rumours were beginning to circulate. At Brandon, during a twenty-minute stop, Rackham cheered up a little after talking to an old settler. The settler described the hard times he'd had, but explained that he had come through all right and told the colonists they'd do the same if they just stuck to it.

After Brandon, the real West began to unfold. Now the colonists gazed out at the empty prairie, the cold brown grass covering the tough sod – flat, treeless, hedgeless as far as the eye could see stretching off to the horizon.

For many this was their first inkling of the future. At last they began to understand what they faced in the land of promise. Here, in this grey realm, the villages – mere clusters of log shacks or hovels of corrugated iron – were dumped down as if by chance. They weren't perched on a hillside or nestled in a valley as in English villages – but stood stark on the level plain.

This was not what they'd expected. But then what *had* they expected? Barr had never told them that the Canadian West was anything like the English countryside. Like the Canadian government's own pamphlets, his had ignored that kind of descriptive detail and talked instead about the promise of the future. He had let the colonists dream their own dreams, and conjure up their own visions. Like all good con men, Barr had allowed them to con themselves.

# CHAPTER FIVE

*Not what they expected*

THE BULK OF THE BARR COLONISTS arrived in Saskatoon on the morning of April 17, 1903, a steaming hot day with a temperature at 85° F (29° C). Barr's agent, the Reverend Dr. Robbins, was there to greet them on the platform and to introduce them to a big broad-shouldered man with a weather-beaten face and brisk moustache. This was Wesley Speers, the colonization agent.

Speers chose the occasion to make a speech, which Stanley Rackham thought was more than a little flowery.

"I have a vision of teeming millions in the great valley to the West where you are going, and you are the forerunners," he cried in his deep voice. "You will not be disappointed. The valley contains the richest land in the Dominion and the Government has provided you with shelter here and will see you safely settled. March westward ho! There are your tents, march!"

The government had been smart enough not to wait for Barr to supply shelter. Instead, Speers had arranged for additional Bell tents and marquees. This was a wise move, because most of Barr's own tents were on the baggage cars running more than a day behind the main trains.

To the newcomers, used to cozy English villages with ivy-covered cottages, Saskatoon looked bleak. Young Paul Hordern was bitterly disappointed. He'd heard a lot about Saskatoon from Canadians at the various stops. "Oh, that's some town," they told him. "That's a big town!" But a big town in Canada wasn't like a big town in the old country. There wasn't even a cobblestone on the wet and muddy main street down which Hordern splashed his way.

Saskatoon was scarcely a year old. It was just another huddle of shacks, with two small hotels, and a few stores – "large boxes rushed up without regard to architecture or comfort," as one newcomer commented. A single stone building, the Windsor Hotel, stood out.

A year before, fewer than one hundred people had lived in the town. Now there were six hundred permanent residents and close to two thousand more passing through. This was the West, raw and new – a few houses clustered around a grain elevator and a railway station, the core of a community no different from scores of others springing up along the rail line.

But Saskatoon, like so many western villages, was on the verge of a boom that would see entire streets built in less than three weeks. Tents began to blossom everywhere. Cowboys, Mounted Police, Indians and Englishmen in broad sombreros crowded its single wooden sidewalk. The atmosphere was that of a lively carnival.

The newcomers had other matters on their minds. Those who had paid four dollars for a tent found now they must pay an extra dollar for shipping costs from Saint John. They began to hold indignation meetings; but Barr hadn't yet arrived in camp so the first meeting came to nothing. They paid their money reluctantly and scheduled a second meeting for Sunday.

By this time they were in another frenzy about their luggage. It finally arrived, jammed into eighteen cars with nobody to sort it out. Some remained on the train. Some

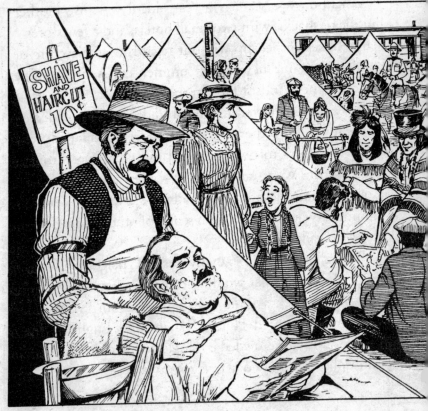

*With its tents and diverse population, Saskatoon took on the atmosphere of a carnival.*

lay in heaps dumped alongside the tracks. Barr now turned up and pleaded for patience. But he made the mistake of warning the crowd the Mounted Police would fire on any who tried to rush the baggage cars. From that point on the wretched clergyman could do nothing right. A brief, wild rush for the baggage cars destroyed the Sunday quiet, blows were struck right and left, and goods captured and retaken.

That Sunday the immigrants jammed into the restaurant marquee and listened to the drone of an Anglican service. Saskatoon had never seen anything like this. A sea

of dainty hats met the eyes of the old-timers as the neatly gloved women in their tailored suits bowed their heads. Beside them, the men mumbled their responses, sober in broadcloth and tweed, with clean shirts, white ties, and neatly polished boots.

The text of the lesson seemed appropriate. It dealt with the rebellion of the children of Israel against Moses. At the same time, here on the Canadian prairies, Barr's children were rebelling against him. The curate read the lesson and described how the rebels were blasted by fire and swallowed by the earth. It was not a passage likely to soothe the rebellious colonists.

Now the minister, Archdeacon Mackay, a veteran of twenty years in the North West, gave as the text for his sermon: "The wilderness and the solitary places shall be glad for them; and the desert shall rejoice and bloom." He welcomed his temporary flock, warned against faint-heartedness, and talked of the pluck and grit needed to make a fortune from Saskatchewan's soil.

Out into the muddy street the congregation poured, with the men in sombreros and fedoras and bowlers, and one even in a silk hat. What a strange spectacle that was! Who but an Englishman would bring a silk hat into the West? It was as if he was walking out into the green and manicured English countryside rather than the yellow prairie.

But of course this was not England. On the west side of the tracks, one hundred acres of white canvas fluttered in the breeze – close to five hundred bell tents and marquees. The tents were pitched every which way in the elbow of the South Saskatchewan, a river red with mud and impossible to reach because of the gigantic blocks of blue ice thrown up on its banks. Scores of men and women were chipping away at these blocks which were the only source of fresh water in the overcrowded community.

Others were struggling to put up more tents, although many had never seen one before. Many more didn't know how to use an axe. A group of Boer War veterans helped these people. And so the Lord's day rolled on, the air alive with the sounds of axe and hammer, wagons creaking and oxen lowing, children crying, men cursing, dogs yapping.

As dusk fell, an ominous glow lit up the sky – not a sunset, but a prairie fire roaring toward the camp. The colonists gaped and wondered. They had never imagined anything like this. Would they be destroyed like the rebellious children of Israel? But village road acted as a fire break, and for the moment at least the newcomers were spared the ravages of nature in the great Northwest.

They were all impatient to get moving towards their new home, but Barr wasn't ready yet. Indignation meetings continued all week. The colonists were furious over the prices charged for food and equipment. But Barr had no control over the Saskatoon merchants who had raised the prices to make an extra dollar.

He tried to escape from one mass meeting, but Wes Speers hauled him back. And there he faced a barrage of questions. Why was he trying to charge his people a guinea each ($50 in today's money) for the privilege of joining the party? Why was he trying to take money from late arrivals for holding their homesteads for them? Why was he charging young girls $10 each for future homesteads? Why was he taking a commission from the leading Saskatoon merchants?

Instead of trying to explain and turn aside these questions, Barr turned ugly. He shouted it was nobody's business, flung out of the tent, and then cried that he wasn't making a cent of profit. He called one man a liar. Pandemonium resulted. Some of the newcomers wanted to toss Barr into the river. Others wanted to kick him out of the camp.

But it must be remembered that many of these complainers were tenderfeet, not used to rough conditions. They tended to magnify the smallest troubles. And they were looking for a scapegoat. Barr provided an easy target. He probably didn't make much out of his project, although he certainly tried. He did receive a 10 percent commission on gold sold to the colonists. He bought oats in town for 40 cents a bushel and sold them for a dollar, when the going rate was only 23½ cents. On his livestock, which he also sold, he got a profit of between twenty and one hundred percent.

Nor did he attempt to calm his critics. A group of colonists asked the member of the North West Territories legislative assembly, James Clinkskill, to discuss the situation in a meeting in the restaurant tent. Barr wouldn't have any of that. He shook his fist in Clinkskill's face and called him an "infamous scoundrel." The meeting broke up as the colonists sang their new song:

> Barr, Barr, wily old Barr
> He'll do as much as he can.
> You bet he will collar
> Your very last dollar
> In the valley of the Sask-atchewan.

Now, Wesley Speers, faced with what he called this "constant turmoil and excitement," realized two things. First, most of the colonists had no farming experience at all. Second, many of them didn't have enough money to run a homestead. Something would have to be done, or the Liberal government would have a political black eye.

Speers took matters into his own hands. He called another meeting to find out who was broke, who needed more money, and who needed to work to earn more. About fourteen hundred people turned out. Speers learned that two hundred had less than ten pounds left apiece. And so he went to work setting up an employment bureau which got jobs for 135 in Moose Jaw, and 50 more in Prince Albert. He got jobs for the rest with local surveying parties, and for the others he arranged practical talks on farming from government inspectors.

By this time the major Canadian newspapers had sent reporters to Saskatoon. The newspapermen were astonished by the naiveté of some of the colonists. The *Toronto News* reported:

"Women who spend their time in dressing and kissing ugly little pug dogs talk of going out to earn money the first year by working in the cornfields, quite blind to the fact that there can be no cornfields there, until they sow the first crop in 1904. A pork packing factory is projected while, as a Westerner points out, there isn't a hog nearer the colony than Battleford."

One western farmer placed in charge of the government horses, J.J. Dodds, was scathing in his criticism. He discovered that not one man in twenty even knew how to hitch up a team. Canadian schoolboys could learn the work faster.

Paul Hordern was convinced that the number of real farmers could be counted on the fingers of one hand. The Horderns decided to leave Barr. A few days after arriving in Saskatoon, they simply packed their goods and located on a homestead near Dundurn, south of Saskatoon.

Mrs. Hordern, who was handling the dry goods store back home in Leicestershire, sold the business and brought the rest of the family out to join her son and husband in 1904. Half a century later, when Saskatchewan celebrated its fiftieth jubilee, Paul Sylvester Hordern was still in Dundurn to join the festivities. He died in Saskatoon in 1983 in his ninety-fifth year.

Not all were as practical as the Horderns. The government and, in fact, the country were beginning to realize that Barr's rosy promises about stout English yeomen were so much eyewash.

The long-suffering government agent, Wes Speers, had his problems. One day in April, while he was working in his tent and planning his employment agency, a thirty-five-year-old Englishman came in, obviously in distress. Behind the Englishman was his wife, slender and dark-eyed, cuddling a tiny fox terrier in her arms. Speers recognized her at once, for she had been the talk of the camp, skipping about, patting her dog, crooning to it as if it were a child. She was clearly a romantic who saw herself as a brave pioneer's wife – a heroine helping her husband to future fortune.

However, her husband was not so optimistic. He had sunk all his money into Barr's failing Stores Syndicate. If he bought a yoke of oxen and a wagon and a breaking plough, he wouldn't have more than seven pounds to his name. "I cannot live on seven pounds for a year and a half," he told Speers. "What am I going to do for food, for a house, for barns and horses?"

"Why, hire yourself out to Mr. Barr to break sod," Speers told him. "Mr. Barr says he'll give you three dollars an acre for the work."

"But I cannot break sod, donchaknow, I never did it before."

"You can learn."

"But where will I live?"

"Build a sod house."

"What's that?"

"A house of sod, built on a ravine side."

"I don't think I could possibly do it."

"Yes, you could. Go ahead and buy your oxen and take your stuff out there. Make some money carrying another man's goods along with you."

"Whom shall I get to drive these oxen?"

"Drive them yourself!"

The Englishman looked dumbfounded.

"Come on down tomorrow and we'll pick out your cattle for you," Speers told him.

She would be kind to the oxen, the wife said. They would be like household pets. She would feed them bread and butter. *Did she say bread and butter?* Yes, she did! A reporter for the *Toronto Star* who had been viewing the scene scribbled those words in his notebook. Speers suppressed a smile. His mind went back to the day when he chased a yoke of oxen up a furrow with a cordwood stick.

"You'll have enough to do to feed yourself bread and butter," he snorted.

"And we shall have some delightful little piggies," she burbled. "I shall go out and bustle in the harvest field with my dear husband." That was too much for Wesley Speers.

"Go and buy those oxen and your plough," he said shortly. "And go ahead if you haven't got a loaf of bread left. The government of this country isn't going to let anybody starve."

There were other bizarre incidents in the tent city as each family bought its equipment and animals and prepared for the long trek to Battleford and then on to the colony. A dozen women cooked for their husbands – all wearing gloves! One six-foot (1.8 m) Englishman washed his fox terrier in a dishpan. One wretched woman, half-drunk, was rescued from the open prairie by the Mounted Police after she had been rushing through the camp shrieking that the Indians had been trying to kidnap her.

And there was more: a crush of three hundred people crammed into the tent post office waiting for the mail; but when it arrived there were only 43 letters. An Englishman was spotted invading the male preserve of the local bar and calling in vain for "an harf 'n harf," a British brew no Canadian had ever heard of. And there was another struggling with an ox, striking it with a sudden fury, then begging the animal's pardon, saying he didn't mean it.

By Friday, April 24, the first colonists were ready to move. But the news wasn't good. Barr's Transportation Syndicate had collapsed. There would be no wagons for the women and children. Charles May, Barr's former agent in Battleford, had quit and was taking up a homestead of his own. And the pioneer party that Barr had sent out to prepare the new site returned in disarray. Its members had lost their way on the prairie, lost their cattle in the muskegs, and starved for three days before reaching civilization.

# Chapter Six

*A trail of fire and blood*

Isaac Barr's original plan had been to establish convoys of twenty or thirty wagons to cover the two-hundred-mile (320 km) distance between Saskatoon and the new colony. The women and children would travel separately. However, the colonists were now striking out on their own without guides.

Each had to find his own way through slough or muskeg and care for his family at nightfall. Many of these were driving horses and oxen for the first time. Some had pocket charts showing that part of the animal's body where the harness could be attached. Others actually used marking chalk to sketch diagrams directly on the horses' sides.

Most spent the best part of a week searching out and bargaining for animals for wagons, for harnesses, farm equipment and supplies. On April 23 the first party got away. The last stragglers didn't set out until May 5. And so, for the best part of a month, the trail that led to Battleford and then westward to the colony was dotted with wagons.

Stanley Rackham had planned to leave on the 23rd, but

*Oxen and carts become mired in the mud on the trail to Battleford.*

he found that the wagon he had chosen had been sold to somebody else. He had to wait until the CPR freight arrived with more. He finally got away at 10 o'clock the following morning, a blistering hot day.

His oxen were soft after an idle winter. He took a long rest at noon, as much for the animals as for himself. By four o'clock he was stuck fast in a bog. A Russian immigrant turned up and helped haul him out. Rackham's experience was repeated again and again that Friday. Even before they found themselves out of sight of Saskatoon, a dozen wagons were stuck in the mud. Matthew Snow, one of the experienced farm instructors hired by the government, helped pull them out.

That was only the beginning. Barr's "road" was nothing more than a deeply rutted trail through the scrub timber made by the Red River carts of the Métis packers bringing in furs from Battleford. The entire country that spring was a heaving bog, dotted by sloughs, little streams and ponds left by the rapidly melting snow.

William Hutchison of Sheffield, whom we last met attending Rev. Lloyd's church service on the *Lake Manitoba,* took the advice of old-timers and delayed his departure until prices came down and the ground was firmer. He was told that a day's delay in Saskatoon would save him two days on the trip, and as a result he and his brother, Ted, reached Battleford without mishap in a fast five days.

Just five miles (8 km) out of Saskatoon, Hutchison came upon four teams of oxen, all stuck fast in the mud.

Exhausted from trying to pull themselves out, they had given up the struggle and were looking around for something to eat. A local farmer took time off from his spring seeding to help haul them free. But Hutchison's own ordeal was yet to come.

The colonists had been warned not to carry more than a thousand pounds (454 kg) per wagon. A team of oxen could manage no more. But most of the carts were overloaded with a ton (907 kg) or a ton and a half (1,360 kg) – even, on occasion, two tons (1,814 kg). Some looked like gigantic Christmas trees, hung with lamps, kitchen chairs, oil cans, baby buggies, plough handles, bags, parcels, tools, women's hats, dogs, and even pianos.

Jolted over the uneven ground, flour sacks burst open and coal oil spilled into the food. The loads were so heavy the women and children had to walk. A bitter wind sprang up. Half an inch (1.3 cm) of ice formed on the ponds. This was the worst spring weather in the memory of the oldest packers. And so the women were forced to trudge numbly onward with the children crying with the cold.

Wagon after wagon sank to its axles in the white alkali mud of the bogs and sloughs. Every time that happened the entire load had to be taken off while the drivers waded through gumbo to find a dry spot. Then the team would be hitched to the rear axle and the wagon hauled out with a logging chain.

These frustrating delays took the best part of a day. There were other problems. The horses, up to their knees in mud, would often lie down and die in the swamps. Many more died from lack of feed or overwork at the hands of men who had never handled a team. One packer counted eighteen dead horses on the trail to Battleford.

A young student missionary, J.A. Donaghy, remembered that "some never seemed to realize how much a horse must eat to live, and the whole country was full of the finest pasture along the trail. It was painful to see horses staggering under the weight of the harness until they dropped." Many horses ran away. Some settlers, afraid of losing their teams, tied them to trees, but with such a short rope they couldn't graze properly and so starved slowly to death.

Barr had planned to have marquees with freshly-baked bread and newly-butchered meat all along the route. That plan collapsed. The government's plan to set up large tents at regular intervals saved a good deal of misery. The first comers crowded in and wolfed tea and porridge, the main food on the trail. The latecomers had to unload and pitch their own tents.

In England it was spring. But here in the Canadian West, blue patches of old snow could still be seen in the bluffs of naked poplars. The settlers grew homesick. Robert Holtby, trudging along mile after mile in the drenching rain – twenty-five miles (40 km) a day behind the family's wagon – thought longingly of the cricket field at home, green as emerald.

Stanley Rackham stared at the brown grass, bleached by the frost, and the gaunt, lifeless trees, and realized that it was May Day back home. And that brought to his mind a familiar vision of primroses, violets, and cowslips surrounding the cottages in his native Mayfield.

But spring was on its way. Water gurgled down the slopes and coulées and into the swelling sloughs, barring the route. For the latecomers there were purple anemones poking out of the grasses. In June the sweet perfume of briar rose filled the night air. Frogs chorused after dark, and wild fowl burst from the willow groves. The crack shots feasted on rabbit, duck, and prairie chicken.

And then suddenly, in the heart of this wilderness, a wilderness of rolling brown hills, white alkali, scrub willow – an astonishing spectacle greeted the trekkers. William Hutchison could scarcely believe his eyes. Here, surrounded by furrowed fields, was a Russian village. Here were houses of trim logs, carefully plastered and neatly arranged along a wide street, their verandahs all gaily painted. This was a Doukhobor settlement, and here the weary travellers rested. The hospitable Slavs took the women and children into their own homes and fed them on fresh eggs and butter.

Hutchison came upon a party of children walking two-by-two to Sunday school. In their brightly-coloured dresses they looked like a living rainbow. He was reminded of a children's ballet at a Christmas pantomime. He and his brother were impressed by the Doukhobors' progress. Here were solid buildings and barns, and droves of fat cattle, and piles of equipment. If these people could make it, so could they! Before they left they took careful note of what they'd seen, storing it in their minds for the day when they might benefit from that lesson.

Not far ahead lay the dreaded Eagle Creek ravine. This was a vast chasm, five miles (8 km) across, with a raging river at the bottom, and sides as steep as the walls of a house. Robert Holtby, gazing at it in awe, thought it must have been torn up by a gigantic earthquake.

Down this dizzy slope ran a bit of a track at an angle so steep it seemed impossible to get down it. Few of the wagons had any brakes. Some of the tenderfeet actually hobbled their oxen before attempting the descent. As a result, the careering wagons rammed into the rumps of the terrified beasts, overturning the whole load, and scattering the contents on the slope. The more experienced drivers locked their rear wheels with chains and stood by with long poles to brake the front wheels should the wagon get away.

The climb upward was equally dismaying. Some wagons required four horses or three teams of oxen to haul the heavy loads up to the rim of the valley. Here, the Holtby family came upon a pitiable sight – a horse had struggled to the top, only to drop dead of fatigue. The ants and hawks were already turning the corpse into a skeleton. By the time the Holtbys reached the government tent at ten that night, young Robert was so tired he could scarcely finish his tea. But the endless squalling of young children kept him awake.

At last they reached Battleford, the mid-way point on

the trail. Here in this historic community, the newcomers got a glimpse of the old west – of fur traders and Indians – now vanishing before the new invasion. Here were the Mounted Police barracks, white and trim, the Hudson's Bay post with its pink roof, and the native school across the river.

The little community, untouched until now by the successive of waves of immigrants, sat on the flat tableland between the North Saskatchewan and Battle Rivers. A government marquee was already in place. The overflow was put up in the nearby agricultural hall. Some of the colonists didn't bother to go any further. They looked for their homesteads in the neighbourhood. Others caught their breath, reorganized their loads, and pressed on to the colony, a hundred miles (160 km) away.

Now they entered wilder country – the empty haunt of Indians and wild animals. Apart from a single farm, there was no white settlement for three hundred miles (480 km) – only rolling hills, little lakes, scrub willow, prairie grass, and pea vine.

Barr had reached Battleford on May 2. That day a large contingent took off for Britannia. Barr spent four days in Battleford, constantly attacked by indignant colonists, many of whom flew into a rage at the mere mention of his name.

The unfortunate clergyman was now seen as a dictator who wanted the absolute right to assign each man a homestead and force him to accept it. Few now believed his shipboard promise that all the land was equal. That was fantasy. Some farms were flat, some were rolling. Some were wooded, some bald. Some were fertile, some stony.

Barr had insisted that all the settlers wait until he personally reached Britannia to dole out homesteads. The Dominion Lands Agent, R.F. Chisholm, told them to ignore that. They could move out of the settlement and find their own land. That angered Barr. "If there's bloodshed and destruction of the colony as a result, I throw the whole blame on you," he shouted at the government man.

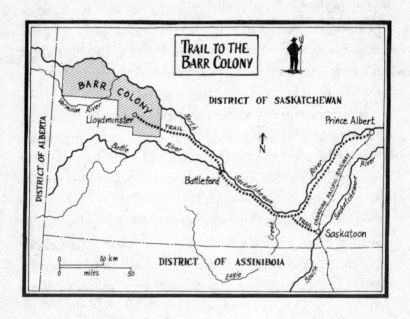

He left for Britannia with Lloyd and, travelling light, reached it on May 9. Lloyd was dismayed by the number of Barr's immigrants who were going back to Battleford in disgust. He began working his way back along the trail to try to talk them out of leaving the colony and going home to England.

These people were bitterly disappointed. They'd reached Britannia ahead of Barr and found nothing there except three large marquees, two of them government tents, the other occupied by Barr's Stores Syndicate. There were no buildings and not a stick of lumber to be had. Despite his promises, Barr had made no arrangement to supply doors and sashes, and float them down the Saskatchewan. There wasn't even a post office. The mail had been dumped on the floor of the stores tent.

The prices the advance party was charging were so high that many packed up and left on the spot – they had bought oats near Battleford at a quarter of the Barr prices.

The only farm in the area, forty miles (64 km) out of Battleford, belonged to Peter Paynter, a ex-Mounted Policeman. For hundreds of outfits strung out along the dreadful trail, this farm was an oasis. Here were herds of horses and cattle, flocks of turkeys, and grunts of pigs. The Holtby family stayed here for two days to give their exhausted horse time to rest. Mrs. Paynter, whose kitchen was full of women and children warming themselves, let Mrs. Holtby use her oven to bake bread while the men put up the tents.

Ahead lay devastation. Fires had charred the land, leaving a wilderness of ruin. No sliver of green could be seen through the black, ashen world that greeted those travellers who'd had the good fortune to escape the flames. Some lost everything – tents, wagons, horses, supplies – everything but their lives.

In this gloomy part of the country, the sloughs and the bogs were the worst the colonists had yet encountered. The Hutchison brothers, who had managed to avoid every swamp on the trail, were stuck fast on three occasions. With their wagon mired to the axles and tilted on its side on the muddy bank of a small torrent, they were struck by a blizzard that blocked their passage for four days.

In all that time they were never dry. Their clothing, greatcoats, and blankets were drenched and encrusted with mud. From Saturday night to the following Thursday they lived on starvation rations: a plate of boiled rice and one pancake made from flour, water, and snow, per meal. When they were able at last to push forward, very little else was moving. They passed scores of tents pitched in the snow beside the trail, their occupants depressed and sick – many of them trying to sell their ploughs and equipment to earn enough to pay for their ticket home.

Meanwhile, at the settlement, Barr became the focus for every complaint. Ivan Crossley watched while one group demanded to know what had happened to all the fresh meat he had promised. At that, Barr seized an axe and knocked down one of his own oxen. "There's fresh meat for you, now!" he cried. "Help yourselves." And they did.

Barr left the colony May 13, taking with him three nurses brought out for the Hospital Syndicate. On May 15 he was back in Battleford, and there he encountered more angry demonstrations. Two Boer War veterans lit into him over their purchase from him of CPR land in the colony. The railway had no record of the transaction. The homesteads had already been sold. Barr blustered, but when threatened with violence he gave them their money back.

It was obvious to all that he *had* been on the make. He'd not only tried to sell supplies at huge prices and collect money for CPR land without approval from the company, but he'd also charged absentee Englishmen $5 apiece to reserve their homesteads. He'd got $10 from single girls in England, promising to settle them later. He'd tried to collect a premium of $5 or more from every settler. He'd taken another $5 from each member of the Hospital Syndicate that he knew was collapsing.

That was the end for Isaac Barr. On May 16, in Battleford, a mass meeting took away any control he had left. Lloyd was appointed in his place as head of a twelve-man committee, quickly dubbed the Twelve Apostles.

In one final moment of bluster Barr shouted that they were all ruffians, and brandished a revolver. But then he meekly gave in, surrendered his records, resigned all claims to a homestead for himself, and turned over everything of value to the community, which all agreed would be named Lloydminster. Barr went back to the settlement where he spent most of his time giving back money to those who felt they'd been cheated. He left forever in mid-June. When he

*In a final moment of bluster, an angry Barr waves a revolver at the colonists.*

reached Regina, he narrowly escaped being pelted by eggs. In Ottawa he tried to get the bonus the government paid to all colonizers, but he was turned down. He was told that he not only caused the government more expense than the total payments would allow, but he'd also tried to squeeze money illegally from British settlers.

That was the end in Canada of Isaac Barr. He married his secretary (his fourth wife, thirty-five years his junior), became an American citizen, and for the rest of his life dreamed unfulfilled dreams of settling people in the far corners of the Empire. He died in Australia in his ninetieth year, still scribbling away in the end papers of a book he was reading, building more imaginary communities in non-existent promised lands.

# CHAPTER SEVEN

~

*Survival*

ALL THE QUALITIES OF THE British in general and the Englishman in particular – their amateurism, their clannishness, their endurance – can be seen in Lloydminster's early years. For Lloydminster was unique. It was the only colony in the West that was 100 percent British. Its leadership was entirely English, its outlook Imperial.

Lloydminster colony started out with everything against it. The leadership was incompetent. The people weren't practical farmers. They refused to learn from other immigrants. And yet in the end it succeeded. There were many reasons for this – the richness of the Saskatchewan River valley, the coming of the Canadian Northern Railway, and the growing prosperity of the Canadian West. But not the least of these reasons was the peculiar English habit of being able to hang on and muddle through.

In exchanging the leadership of Isaac Barr for that of the Reverend Mr. George Exton Lloyd and his twelve-man committee, the colonists weren't out of the woods. Lloyd was likeable but hopelessly incompetent. George Langley, the land agent, called the twelve apostles "one of the most incapable bodies of men that ever got together." J.A. Donaghy described Lloyd as "the blind leading the blind."

Speers reported an absence of all business methods among Lloyd and his council. The hospital plan collapsed. The Stores Syndicate went out of business. Free enterprise replaced the cooperative effort. Power went to Lloyd's head and he became a dictator.

One problem was Lloyd's super patriotism. He and his committee insisted that nobody except Englishmen would be allowed to settle in the colony. That was Barr's original plan. He had written, "We hope to keep the colony free from any foreign admixture, even of American people.... I think it not wise to mix that people with this colony. I hope to keep it British in actuality as well as in settlement."

As a result, the English tenderfeet had no practical farmers from Iowa and Nebraska as neighbours to help them by example and advice. The colony's doctor, who stayed behind when the Hospital Syndicate folded, found his work was constant but pretty monotonous. His biggest daily chore was stitching up axe wounds. Scores of colonists had never before had an axe or hatchet in their hands.

This lack of experience and of knowledgeable neighbours held up the colony's development for at least a year and caused untold hardships. Some of the buildings being erected on the homesteads were among the poorest in the Northwest. Some were almost useless. Many were so badly built the roofs were in danger of collapsing.

To understand the problem facing these green arrivals, let us go out into the empty prairie with Ivan Crossley and see what he and his Irish friends were up against.

The land agent brought them here, located the survey posts and left them standing behind their wagon on their new homestead – 640 acres (260 hectares) of unbroken prairie, some twelve miles (19 km) southeast of the colony. What a lonely scene this was! There wasn't a sign of human habitation – nothing as far as the eye could see except for the prairie blackened by fire, and a few skeletal clumps of charred cottonwood.

The scene was not unique. It had already been repeated thousands of times in the open country that lay between the Red River and Rockies. It would be repeated thousands of times more before the plains were broken and fenced, and would remain engraved on Ivan Crossley's memory for all of his life, as well as on the memories of thousands of others – British, American, German, Scandinavian, Slav, and Dutch. None would ever forget those first despairing moments on the limitless ocean of the prairie.

This was home. This was where they must live. This hard turf on which they stood – as tough as human gristle – would be their building material. Before they could prosper, before they could plant a single grain, they would have to attack it, break it, turn it over, rip it apart, and finally nurture the black soil beneath. That became the folk memory of the West.

Crossley knew that some of their compatriots faced

a challenge had already packed up and fled. He and his partners were almost broke. But they didn't have wives or children, they had enthusiasm and energy, and they were young. And so they pitched their tent, unloaded their walking plough, and went to work.

They had a sketchy idea of how to build a sod house. So they set to work ploughing long strips of various lengths, dragging them to the site on a stone boat of fire-killed trees. They learned by trial and error. The house would be sixteen by twelve feet (4.8 by 3.6 m). They simply marked out a space, laid a row of sods along it, and kept on building until the walls were eight feet (2.4 m) high.

There would be no windows – they couldn't get any glass. But they made a door out of split poles, and they covered it with blankets. They made a kind of roof out of small poplar poles, laid close together and shaped to shed the rain. They piled more sods on top of the poles and chinked them with earth. That would have to do – even though it wasn't watertight. But then, no sod house was. There was a saying in the West that if it rained three days outside, it rained for two weeks inside. They would have to get used to that.

They installed their stove, built bunks out of more poles, and made mattresses of branches. As Crossley said, it would take a lot of imagination to call this hovel a house. But it would be their only shelter in the winter to come, and before many weeks crept by they would start to think of it as home.

It was one thing, of course, to throw up a house of sorts, but quite another to begin practical farming. Crossley and his friends tried to plant a garden in a bare spot where the sods had been stripped away, only to discover too late that they had removed the best soil. The vegetables withered and died and the men were forced to go to work for wages.

Scores left the colony to seek jobs. Scores more would have gone had Lloyd and his committee not persuaded them to stay, promising jobs in the town itself, jobs that never appeared. Others sat in their homesteads trying to break up the land with little success.

Matthew Snow, the government farm inspector, had great trouble getting the colonists to move quickly to break the land and get it ready for the following year's crops. The breaking season was quickly passing and yet seventy percent had no chance of getting a crop in the following year let alone in that summer of 1903. Teams stood idle, some animals straying away because their owners were so lazy. They didn't seem to realize the prairie could be broken only in the summer. Many thought, in their ignorance, that they could work late in the fall, after their houses were finished.

In fact, these middle-class Englishmen from Leeds and Birmingham, London and Manchester, had no comprehension of the harshness of the prairie climate. They'd never known a western winter. They'd never faced a blizzard or a whiteout. They'd never felt their eyelids freeze together, or their skin peel off when they pressed it against icy metal. The Slavs and Scandinavians, the Nebraskans and Iowans were used to this. The Englishmen weren't. By fall it was clear that the average amount of farmland broken by the plough, let alone planted, was less than two acres (0.8 hectares) a homestead.

That winter, in the course of a snowshoe patrol, Sergeant D.J. McCarthy of the Mounted Police came upon a queer scene some miles to the southeast of Lloydminster. Here he found one of the colonists, crouched in his shack with the door partly open, sitting close to his stove, wearing all his outer clothing, including his cap and mitts, and calmly reading Shakespeare.

The door wouldn't close because he'd pushed a long tree from the outside into the door of the stove. When the fire died down, he just pushed the tree farther in. He seemed quite cheerful, and invited the policeman in for a spot of tea, and explained that he was the son of a former British ambassador to Turkey.

In sharp contrast was the example of those who *had* farming experience. They did well. By July 22, William Rendell, whose family had farmed in England for two centuries, managed to break and plant three acres (1.2 hectares) of oats, an acre and a half (0.6 hectares) of barley, another acre and a half of potatoes, and a quarter acre (0.1 hectares) of vegetables. His family bungalow, the largest of the settlement, was within two weeks of completion, even though Rendell had to haul the lumber thirty miles (48 km).

But Rendell was one of the few who knew his business.

He'd refused the homestead Barr had offered, had chosen another one, and started to plough the day after he got there. That winter his wife, Alice, wrote her friends in England an enthusiastic letter, in which she said, "I would never advise anyone to come out here who is afraid of work. They are better off at home. There is room to breathe in this country and if the work is hard the freedom, which is the indispensable attribute of the life here, makes one far less susceptible to physical fatigue.... Here one feels that each week's work is a step forward whilst in the old country oftentimes a year's hard work brought nothing but disappointment...."

The Rendells were in a minority. Less than 10 percent of the people had farming experience. Wesley Speers called a meeting to see who needed government aid, but was hampered by the pride of the English. As one woman told him: "I will not become the object of charity."

He was appalled at the conditions among the destitute. The worst example was that of J.G. Bulmer, whose ailing wife was the mother of eighteen children, one no more than three weeks old. While Speers was visiting the family, she fainted dead away. Bulmer had a fine piece of land, but he hadn't broken a foot of ground, so Speers packed the entire family off to Battleford.

An equally pathetic case was that of Alexander Carlyle-Bell, who had somehow dropped his wallet, stuffed with $200 in cash, on the prairie and then lost a bank draft for $500. The wretched man could do nothing right. He'd managed to break seven acres (2.8 hectares) on a quarter-section of land, only to discover it was the *wrong* section. The last straw came when his wife fell off the wagon and broke her arm. That was the last the colony saw of the Carlyle-Bells.

And yet the settlers muddled through – and somehow they made it through the winter. Some men took jobs during the cold weather, not always successfully. Speers was frustrated at the settlers' ineptitude. By the following spring very little land was broken. Three-quarters of the horses were dead of exposure, and the rest were ailing.

Speers was fed up with Lloyd and his committee, who thought in city terms rather than country terms. Speers was convinced Lloyd and his council were wasting the colonists' time at the planting season with endless meetings, organizations and sub-committees. They were all planning in a most optimistic fashion for a glorious future – discussing taxes and lot sizes and all the details of municipal organization, "troubling about small things that should give them no concern ... trying to build up a commerce without cultivating their good lands...."

Speers himself was a rugged and practical farmer, but his patience was sorely tried. Like all Canadians, he'd welcomed the British. But now, in their own way, they were proving a maddening group. What were they doing, organizing musical societies, tennis clubs, theatrical performances, and literary circles in the town, when they ought to be in the fields, building up their quarter-sections? In

Speers's view, they couldn't afford such indulgence. What these people lacked, he thought, was not culture, but common sense.

Yet they were beginning to prosper. The impossible cases had been weeded out. Those left behind were learning slowly by trial and error. In 1905 they broke more land than they had during the previous two years combined.

By November Lloyd was out of the way – promoted to Archdeacon of Prince Albert. Now there arrived in the area a group of Americans and Canadians with farming experience. And that fall of 1905 the Canadian Northern Railway arrived at last.

By February of 1907, the local immigration agent was able to report that Lloydminster had surpassed all expectations. In 1908, the Lloydminster board of trade felt justified in putting out a pamphlet boosting the town as "the Banner District of the West."

By that time all the heartache and controversy that had marked the settlement's early days were forgotten. As one old-timer put it many years later, "Strangely enough, as the years rolled by, it was apparent that several among the most successful settlers were men with no previous farming experience."

That was certainly true of William Hutchison, who, by 1905, was able to write an article on "How to Become a Farmer" for his hometown paper in England. Stanley Rackham was another who did well. In fact he could have afforded to make regular trips home to the old country.

But he never left the site of the Barr Colony, and he was still in Lloydminster in 1937 when he died at the age of sixty.

Like many others, Ivan Crossley alternately farmed his homestead and added to his income by taking temporary jobs. When he needed money, he'd go to work ploughing another man's field, or taking a winter mail contract from Battleford or Saskatoon. In between he'd go back to his homestead, break ground, work on his shack, put up a barn, until he owned the land outright.

In 1906 Crossley ran into his former shipmate, Robert Holtby, bringing a load of hay into town for sale. Robert Holtby's pretty sister was sitting astride the load. Crossley took her to lunch and soon became a regular visitor at the thriving Holtby homestead, seven miles (11 km) out of town. The pair were engaged that fall, and married in Lloyd's log church the following spring. They enjoyed forty-eight years of married life – the memories of those early struggles on the long trail from Saskatoon slowly fading as the years wore on and Lloydminster prospered and the grandchildren of that pioneer union began to arrive.

# INDEX

Coming Soon

## STEEL ACROSS THE PLAINS

William Cornelius Van Horne was the greatest railway man
in North America. As the energetic chairman of the Canadian Pacific Railway (CPR), it was his job to ensure that a
ribbon of steel would be laid down between Winnipeg and
Calgary in record time. It was an epic, back-breaking task,
involving more than 7,000 men and 2,000 teams of horses
and spanning 1,000 kilometres. By the end of 1883, the
railroad was a reality on the prairie. Soon towns with names
such as Moose Jaw and Swift Current were dotting the map.

In *Steel Across the Plains,* Pierre Berton vividly recreates
the events that opened the West to white settlers — and sig-
nalled the end of the traditional native way of life.